Original title:
Rising Through Pain

Copyright © 2024 Swan Charm
All rights reserved.

Author: Paulina Pähkel
ISBN HARDBACK: 978-9916-89-607-5
ISBN PAPERBACK: 978-9916-89-608-2
ISBN EBOOK: 978-9916-89-609-9

The Canvas of Survival

In shadows deep, we find our way,
Colors blend, come what may.
With every stroke, a story told,
Crafting strength from purest gold.

Beneath the weight of heavy skies,
Hope ignites, and never dies.
Each battle fought, each tear we shed,
Turns pain to art, where dreams are fed.

In whispered winds, a promise gleams,
A canvas woven with our dreams.
While storms may rage and tempests roar,
We paint our truth, forevermore.

Through shadows cast by doubt and fear,
Resilience blooms, it draws us near.
With every hue, we make our stand,
Unfurling life, hand in hand.

The canvas broad, our spirits soar,
In every challenge, we explore.
United in hues both dark and bright,
We sculpt our journey, chase the light.

Between Burdens and Blessings

In the quiet of dawn's embrace,
We balance life at a steady pace.
Weights of worries, joys unfold,
Moments cherished, stories told.

Burdens heavy yet blessings sweet,
In harmony, they intertwine, meet.
With every step, we find a grace,
A tender smile upon our face.

Life a ledger of highs and lows,
Between the chaos, soothing flows.
In trials faced, we find our song,
Together where we all belong.

Through tangled paths and winding roads,
We learn to carry, share the loads.
Hearts resilient, spirits bright,
Guided gently by the light.

So let us dance in twilight's glow,
Between what's lost and what we know.
For in this weave, our truths align,
In burdens shared, a blessing shines.

The Strength of Silent Cries

In shadows deep, a voice unheard,
Whispers echo, silent, stirred.
Within the heart, a battle rages,
Strength unfolds through silent pages.

The weight we bear, a heavy cloak,
Yet from our pain, a flame bespoke.
With every sigh, we rise again,
From quiet hurt, we'll break the chain.

Beneath the surface, spirits soar,
In quiet strength, we find the core.
These silent cries, a warrior's song,
In hearts of silence, we grow strong.

Resilience blooms in shaded light,
Fighting darkness with inner might.
For every tear, a seed is sown,
In silent battles, we've beautifully grown.

Phoenix in the Night

From ashes cold, a flame ignites,
In darkest hours, the heart takes flight.
Rising anew with wings ablaze,
Through struggles fierce, we learn to praise.

The night is long, but hope shall bloom,
Defying fate, dispersing gloom.
A phoenix born from loss and fire,
With every fall, we climb up higher.

Transformation's power lies within,
In chaos swirls, we find our kin.
When shadows loom, and dreams feel tight,
We stretch and soar, a fearless sight.

In whispered winds, our spirits sing,
Embracing change, we take to wing.
Eternal flight from dusk till dawn,
A phoenix rises, reborn, withdrawn.

Through the Cracks of Stone

In rocky paths, a seed finds light,
Through cracks of stone, it claims its right.
With gentle strength, it breaks the mold,
In toughened ground, a story told.

The earth may harden, yet life persists,
Through grit and grind, the green insists.
A single sprout, defying odds,
Emerging strong against the gods.

Resilience thrives in risky space,
Beneath the stone, the roots embrace.
Hope creeps in where none would dare,
Through trials brave, we learn to share.

Let nature teach us to be bold,
For strength is found in stories old.
From every crack, new life breaks free,
In stone and struggle, we find glee.

The Beauty in Bruises

In shades of blue and hints of brown,
The beauty lies beneath the frown.
Marks of battles, life's embrace,
Stories captured, time's gentle trace.

Each bruise a tale, each scar a song,
In pain we find a place to belong.
With every hurt, we stitch our seams,
The strength within, a world of dreams.

Against the odds, we learn to rise,
In colors deep, the truth defies.
Embrace the flaws, the battles fought,
In every bruise, a lesson taught.

Through trials faced, our hearts will bloom,
Emerging bold from quiet doom.
In life's canvas, dark and bright,
We find the beauty in our fight.

Unyielding through the Years

Time drips like rain, soft yet clear,
Memories linger, held so dear.
Roots grow deeper, seasons change,
Strength found in the midst of pain.

Through the storms, we bend and sway,
But like the trees, we find our way.
Holding steadfast, hearts ablaze,
We learn to dance in life's harsh maze.

Whispers of hope, they guide the night,
Carrying dreams, our guiding light.
A journey marked by scars and tears,
Unyielding spirits through the years.

In shadows cast, we seek the sun,
Striding forward, we won't run.
Gathering strength from days gone by,
With every leap, we touch the sky.

In every heartbeat, every breath,
Resilience lingers, conquering death.
We stand together, hand in hand,
Unyielding still, a vibrant band.

Embers of the Forgotten

Flickering softly, these embers glow,
Ghosts of the past in the night's flow.
Each spark a story, a silence kept,
Whispers of dreams that we've all wept.

Under the ash, a warmth resides,
Crimson flickers where memory hides.
Fragments of laughter, shades of pain,
Woven together like threads of rain.

Forgotten tales beneath the fire,
Echoes of hearts, consumed by desire.
In darkened corners, stories dwell,
Eager to rise, to break their shell.

A dance of shadows, a flick of flame,
Rekindling the lost, restoring the name.
Embers whisper from ages past,
Lighting the night, hope unsurpassed.

With each soft glow, we learn to see,
The beauty hidden in what used to be.
From ashes, new dreams ignite the morn,
Embers of the forgotten reborn.

The Mirror of My Struggles

Reflecting back through shattered glass,
Each crack a tale of moments past.
In the depths of hardship, strength is found,
Lessons carved deep within the ground.

Fighting demons, wrestling fears,
Every drop of sweat tells of years.
With every bruise, a story is spun,
In the mirror's glare, we've already won.

Fragments of growth lies in each tear,
Embracing courage, we persevere.
In the glint of doubt, hope will appear,
Showing the path we are meant to steer.

Each reflection, a battle we've faced,
In the starlit struggle, our spirit's traced.
Through wild chaos, we find our song,
A melody of righting the wrong.

So stare into the mirror's night,
Find your strength, let it ignite.
In every challenge, we rise again,
The mirror holds truths we can't pretend.

Heartbeats after Heartbreak

In silence echoes, the heart's refrain,
A melody played from longing pain.
With every beat, a whisper calls,
Even in sorrow, hope never falls.

Cracked foundations may seem so stark,
Yet from the ashes, we kindle a spark.
With each exhale, we breathe anew,
Finding the rhythm in love's overdue.

Heartbeats pulse through sleepless nights,
A tender war within the fights.
Yet in the struggle lies the grace,
Resilience wrapped in each embrace.

Remembering joys that once did bloom,
Through heavy clouds, we find room.
Each heartbeat sings a story told,
The beauty found as we grow old.

So let the echoes ring so clear,
For after heartbreak, love draws near.
In every heartbeat that we keep,
Awakens dreams that once were deep.

From Tears to Triumph

Tears flowed like rain, soft and pure,
Each drop held a dream, a heart's allure.
Yet from the sorrow, strength would rise,
A dawn would break through stormy skies.

With every struggle, shadows fade,
In the light of hope, fears are laid.
Victory whispers with a gentle tone,
From tears to triumph, we have grown.

The path is steep, the journey long,
But in the silence, we find our song.
Together we stand, hands held tight,
In the embrace of love, we ignite.

Through valleys deep and mountains high,
With every challenge, we learn to fly.
In the dance of life, we face the fight,
From tears to triumph, hearts take flight.

With courage as our guiding star,
We've come so far, we know who we are.
In every heartbeat, there's a story spun,
From tears to triumph, we have won.

The Path of the Unyielding

In storms of doubt, we find our way,
The path ahead is where we stay.
With every step, the ground may shake,
But hearts keep marching, for hope's sake.

Beneath the weight of shadows cast,
We carry dreams from the past.
The burdens heavy, yet spirits light,
Each challenge met brings forth new light.

Through thorns and brambles, we will tread,
With courage forged, no fear in dread.
In unity strong, we rise and sing,
The path of truth gives us our wings.

Though rivers may swell and winds may howl,
Together we stand, through every scowl.
For in the heart of the storm, we find
The path of the unyielding is entwined.

Strength flows from every tear we've shed,
In the face of trial, we are led.
With every heartbeat, we reclaim our fate,
The path of the unyielding, strong and great.

Notes of a Greater Symphony

In the quiet whispers of the night,
Notes of dreams take graceful flight.
Melodies echo in hearts' embrace,
Creating warmth, a sacred space.

With every chord, a story unfolds,
A tapestry woven, bright and bold.
In harmony found, our spirits soar,
In the symphony of life, we explore.

Each note, a journey, each pause, a breath,
In rhythm of life, we dance with death.
Yet through the chaos, a truth remains,
In notes of joy, we heal our pains.

The silence speaks in echoes clear,
Inviting us to draw near.
In every heartbeat, in every sigh,
Notes of a greater symphony fly.

With hands joined together, we play our parts,
Creating a masterpiece with our hearts.
In unity's song, we find our plea,
Notes of a greater symphony, wild and free.

Shields Made of Solitude

In the stillness, shadows breathe,
Thoughts like whispers, they weave and seethe.
Solitude, a gentle friend at dusk,
In her embrace, we learn to trust.

With every moment spent alone,
We carve our strength from silent stone.
In solitude's arms, wounds begin to mend,
The heart finds solace, time to transcend.

Though the world may rush and voices clash,
In quietude, fierce spirits flash.
Here we build our fragile shields,
With every truth that solitude yields.

Amidst the chaos, a fortress stands,
Crafted from dreams and tender hands.
While others may fear the quiet's beam,
In solitude's glow, we find our dream.

Through the lens of silence, we see our light,
Shields made of solitude, burning bright.
In moments alone, we gather the stars,
Finding courage and peace that's truly ours.

Climbing through the Dark

With every step, a whisper calls,
Through shadows deep, where silence falls.
A flicker glows, a guiding light,
As courage blooms amidst the night.

Each handhold scarce, yet strong we climb,
Though fears may rise, we conquer time.
The summit waits—a breath away,
In darkness found, we seize the day.

The path is steep, the weight is soul,
Yet still we rise, we seek the whole.
With every challenge, bonds grow tight,
Together we ascend the height.

When Hope Blooms in the Gloom

In the deepest night, a seed is sown,
In barren lands, where cold winds moan.
A tender shoot breaks through despair,
Its petals stretch, perfuming air.

With each new dawn, the darkness fades,
What once was lost, anew cascades.
The colors burst, a vivid scene,
Where love and faith have always been.

When shadows cling and spirits tire,
A flicker grows, igniting fire.
Together, hearts can brave the gloom,
In every heart, hope finds a room.

Lanterns in the Storm

When winds collide, the night is fierce,
Candles flicker, their glow to pierce.
Each lantern hangs on willow's grace,
A beacon bright in dark's embrace.

Through thunder's roar and lightning's flash,
We find our calm, our spirit's stash.
With every gust, we stand as one,
In tempest's heart, our love's begun.

The storm may rage, yet here we stand,
Together strong, hand in hand.
Each lantern's glow, a promise true,
That brighter days are born anew.

Every Scar a Story

Upon the skin, the tales we write,
Of battles fought in day and night.
Each scar a mark of survival's grace,
In every line, a memory's trace.

The heart knows well the weight of pain,
Yet through the hurt, we grow again.
With every scratch, a lesson learned,
The fire within, forever burned.

Through life's cruel hand and tender touch,
Each scar reminds us we are such.
Brave souls weaving through the fray,
Every scar a part of the way.

The Resurgent Flame

In the darkest night, a spark will glow,
A flicker of hope, bold and aglow.
Through ashes and doubt, it dances bright,
A flame reborn, in the heart of night.

With every gust, it sways and bends,
A testament deep, where despair ends.
Fanning the embers, a passion ignites,
The resurgent flame, a beacon in sights.

Against the cold winds, it fiercely fights,
In shadows of doubt, it claims its rights.
Through trials and tears, it stands so tall,
The resurgent flame, it won't let us fall.

So let it blaze on, through time and space,
In each beating heart, find its embrace.
For courage and hope will always remain,
In the heart that beats with a resurgent flame.

Whispered Wins in the Wind

The gentle breeze carries tales of cheer,
Of dreams fulfilled, and hopes held dear.
With every sigh, the world takes flight,
Whispered wins in the soft twilight.

Across the fields, the daisies dance,
Each petal a note in a sweet romance.
With laughter entwined in rustling leaves,
The heart finds solace, and courage believes.

Through mountains high and valleys wide,
The whispers guide us, with love as our stride.
In every moment, a story to see,
Whispered wins, set the spirit free.

The wind its canvas, painting the sky,
With trials faced and dreams to fly.
So listen closely, let your heart mend,
For hope whispers softly in every bend.

Storms and Stars

When storms arise and shadows fall,
The heart may tremble, yet still stand tall.
For every tempest, there's strength bestowed,
In darkened skies, true colors showed.

Through thunder's roar and lightning's flash,
The spirit bends, refusing to crash.
In chaos' grip, a dance unfolds,
As courage burns brighter than gold.

Then after the rain, the stars appear,
A reminder that light can conquer fear.
Their twinkle tells of the storms bygone,
In every struggle, we learn to carry on.

So face the tempest, embrace the night,
For storms will pass, revealing the light.
In the balance of chaos, we find our way,
Through storms and stars, we grow every day.

Notes of a Resilient Heart

In quiet moments, the heart will sing,
Of battles fought and the strength they bring.
With every bruise, a lesson learned,
Notes of resilience, in fire burned.

Through tears and trials, we rise anew,
With courage woven in each shade of blue.
In the darkest times, a promise made,
To stand with grace, unafraid, unshayed.

The rhythm pulses, a steady beat,
In shadows long, the heart won't retreat.
With every heartbeat, a tale unfolds,
Of bravery fierce, and love that holds.

From sorrow's depths to peaks of delight,
The resilient heart will shine so bright.
Through every storm, through every tear,
It sings a song, enchanting, clear.

Beyond the Depths

In shadows deep where silence reigns,
Whispers linger, breaking chains.
The heartache flows like silent streams,
Yet hope will rise from shattered dreams.

In the abyss where fears take flight,
We seek the truth in endless night.
Emerging from the darkened maze,
We find the strength to face the blaze.

With every wave that crashes bold,
The tales of courage start to unfold.
We learn to swim in stormy seas,
And in the depths, we find our keys.

So journey on, oh soul so bright,
Illuminate the darkest night.
For in the depths, we learn to see,
The beauty born of misery.

Lessons from the Abyss

In silence deep, the lessons stir,
From shadows cast, we start to learn.
The void that swallows light away,
Holds truths we must not disobey.

Each tear that falls, a weight we bear,
In darkest nights, we learn to care.
Through pain and doubt, a fire ignites,
Guiding us through the endless fights.

From whispered thoughts, to screams unheard,
A symphony in pain, absurd.
Yet wisdom blooms where fears reside,
In depths of struggle, we abide.

We chart our course through murky tides,
In every loss, a lesson bides.
Embrace the scars that time has drawn,
For in the night, new paths are spawned.

Through Thorns to Bloom

In gardens filled with jagged thorns,
We find the light in hearts reborn.
A tender shoot defies the strife,
Emerging strong, it claims its life.

With every bruise, a lesson learned,
From shadows cast, new fires burned.
Resilience grows where pain has sown,
In cracked foundations, seeds are thrown.

The sun will shine on tender blooms,
Transforming whispers into tunes.
Through trials faced, the spirit shines,
In vibrant hues, the heart entwines.

So let us tread through thorny ways,
For in the struggle, beauty lays.
Each wound a chapter, each bruise a spark,
In fragrant gardens born from dark.

Timeless Tales of the Torn

In stories old, where hearts have bled,
We weave the fabric, thread by thread.
The tales of loss, the whispers share,
Of fragile souls, laid bare, aware.

Each chapter penned with tears of gold,
In the pages worn, the truth unfolds.
With every scar, a story's spun,
Of battles lost, and victories won.

Through storms we rise, through fires we learn,
In every fracture, we brightly burn.
For every tale of heartache told,
A legacy of strength unfolds.

So gather close, hear voices past,
In timeless tales, our bonds hold fast.
From wounds once torn, new dreams will soar,
In whispered echoes, forevermore.

Shadows that Speak

In the quiet of the night,
Shadows dance through the air.
Whispers echo softly here,
Tales of life, love, and despair.

Darkness shapes their silent forms,
Relics of the past emerge.
Each flicker tells a story,
A longing, an urge to purge.

Underneath the silver moon,
They sway with a gentle grace.
Transforming fear into dreams,
In this sacred, hidden space.

Hear the voices in the gloom,
Each shadow has its own refrain.
In the depths, they find connection,
A bond formed through shared pain.

Carry forth their words tonight,
Let them guide you on your way.
For in shadows, we may find,
The light that leads to brighter days.

Currents of Healing

Gentle waves caress the shore,
Like whispers of soothing grace.
Each drop holds a promise true,
Bringing strength to the weary place.

In the depths, the pain resides,
Yet the river flows with zeal.
It carries hope for every heart,
A powerful force to heal.

The ebb and flow of life's own song,
Reminds us we're never alone.
With each current, a breath of peace,
Our spirits rise, our worries flown.

From the mountains to the sea,
Nature's gift is clear and bright.
In every ripple, find your calm,
Embrace the power of soft light.

Let the waters wash your fears,
Let them soothe your troubled mind.
In these currents, find your worth,
A sacred journey, intertwined.

Artistry in Struggles

Canvas stretched beneath the stars,
Colors blend in twilight's hue.
Each stroke a story from the heart,
Crafted by the brave and true.

Layers deep, the pain reveals,
Yet beauty rises from the dust.
In the midst of chaos, find,
A masterpiece built on trust.

Brush and pen, tools of the soul,
Chisel life into the stone.
From struggles born an art divine,
Transforming sorrow into tone.

Each imperfection plays its part,
A melody of what has been.
With every flaw, a work of art,
The heart beats strong beneath the skin.

Reclaim the night, embrace the fight,
Find the grace in every fall.
For in the artistry of strife,
We rise to answer the call.

Breath of the Brave

In the silence before dawn,
Courage whispers soft and low.
Take a breath, face the unknown,
Let your heart's true strength bestow.

With each inhale, gather fire,
Exhale doubts that linger long.
Let the spirit lead the way,
Through the challenges, be strong.

The journey may be winding,
A path marked by fear and grace.
Breathe in deep, embrace the light,
Stand your ground, hold your place.

Moments lost and moments found,
Each heartbeat melds into one.
With the breath of every warrior,
A legacy can be spun.

Bravery is not the absence,
Of the doubts that fill the mind,
But the choice to keep on moving,
With an open heart, aligned.

The Dance of Defiance

In shadows where the brave ignite,
They twirl with flames, refusing fright.
A step, a leap, against the norm,
In chaos, they embrace the storm.

With every spin, a voice declared,
In rhythm, all their burdens bared.
They break the chains that hold them tight,
And claim their claim, their fierce birthright.

With eyes ablaze, they dare to dream,
A dance of hope, a vibrant theme.
In sync with beats of hearts so bold,
Their stories etched in glimmers gold.

They twine with fate, a daring waltz,
In unison, they find their faults.
From ashes rise, in fearless grace,
A tapestry of worlds they face.

So let them whirl, let passions soar,
In defiance, they forever roar.
For in this dance, the spirits thrive,
A celebration—brave and alive.

Emblem of Endurance

Through trials faced, their spirits bend,
With scars and tales that never end.
They stand as mountains, tall and proud,
In silence strong, they speak aloud.

Each drop of sweat, a badge of fight,
A testament to endless night.
With whispered dreams, they pave the way,
In shadows deep, they find their sway.

Like rivers flow, they carve their paths,
In stormy seas, they face the wrath.
Resilience blooms in barren lands,
With steady hearts and steady hands.

Through tempests fierce, they forge ahead,
With every bruise, their glory spread.
In whispers soft, they lift the veils,
And in their strength, the world exhales.

For they are more than weary souls,
A saga told where courage rolls.
An emblem worn through harshest fights,
They glow like stars in darkest nights.

Threads of a Tattered Heart

In woven seams of love once strong,
Rippling echoes of a lost song.
Frayed edges tell of time's cruel art,
Each tear a tale of a tattered heart.

With colors bright now dulled by tears,
The fabric worn through countless years.
Yet through the holes, light filters in,
A gentle warmth beneath the skin.

Each knot a memory sketched in pain,
Transforming sorrow into gain.
With threads entwined, hope's whisper starts,
Repatching dreams of broken parts.

In motley forms, they intertwine,
Through every stitch, the threads align.
They craft anew from faded hues,
Reviving love in vibrant clues.

So mend the seams, embrace the scars,
Let healing light shine like the stars.
For every stitch, a journey's mark,
Threads of a heart that lights the dark.

Healing with a Heavy Heart

With gentle hands, they cradle pain,
In quiet spaces, grief's refrain.
A heavy heart, an aching soul,
Yet in their depths, they find a whole.

Each breath a step through mending streams,
In darkness, hope begins to gleam.
The weight may rest upon their chest,
But through each trial, they find their rest.

They carve the silence with soft sighs,
In every moment, time defies.
For healing takes its own sweet time,
In rhythmic beats, a subtle rhyme.

The burdens carried, yet they rise,
With strength anew, beneath the skies.
Embracing all that life has churned,
A lesson learned, a heart returned.

For with the weight, there comes the flight,
In shadows cast, they find the light.
Healing blooms where pain once reigned,
A heavy heart, uniquely claimed.

The Symphony of the Strong

In shadows deep, the bold arise,
With hearts of steel and open skies.
They dance through storms, ignite the night,
Chasing dreams with fierce delight.

A symphony of hopes unbound,
With every note, a strength profound.
Together they lift, together they soar,
In harmony's grip, they seek and explore.

From trials faced, their spirits gleam,
Resilient souls that dare to dream.
Through every setback, they find their song,
A chorus of courage, forever strong.

With voices united, they rise as one,
Transforming darkness into sun.
In the symphony's heart, they beat and blow,
Creating a melody only they know.

Celebrating life with every chord,
In rhythms pure, their spirits adored.
They stand with pride, hand in hand,
In the symphony of the strong, they stand.

Paths carved in Pain

Through jagged stones, the footsteps lead,
Each mark a tale, every struggle a seed.
In valleys low, their shadows loom,
A testament to overcoming gloom.

The roads are rough, the nights are long,
Yet in their hearts, they hum a song.
A melody born from scars and strife,
Each note a whisper of their life.

In silence deep, they find their way,
Navigating through the disarray.
With every tear, a lesson learned,
In ashes cold, their passion burned.

From wounds made whole, they rise anew,
Building paths with the strength they drew.
Though pain may linger, they won't retreat,
Each step forward, a victory sweet.

With courage born from broken chains,
They walk the paths carved in pain.
In the nights of trial, light will reign,
For in each journey, they'll find their gain.

Transitions of the Tethered

In bonds unseen, they learn to grow,
Within the ties that ebb and flow.
From rooted fears to soaring heights,
They seek the dawn, embrace the lights.

Through whispered doubts, and gentle pulls,
They navigate with hearts so full.
In every change, they find their rhyme,
The tether strong, a dance through time.

As seasons shift, their colors blend,
Finding hope in the turns that bend.
In the currents of love, they drift and sway,
With every heartbeat, a brand new way.

The tether tight, yet free to roam,
In every leap, they find their home.
With courage fueling their guided flight,
They transition boldly towards the light.

In the tapestry of their shared embrace,
Each moment cherished, each line a trace.
Through transitions vast, they softly tether,
In harmony's bond, they're light as feather.

From Grief to Grace

In shadow's clutch, the heart does ache,
With every tear, a soul to break.
Yet in the depths of sorrow's claim,
A flicker waits, the spirit's flame.

Through heavy rains, the heart will wade,
In solitude, bonds of love are made.
With whispered hopes, they lift the veil,
From anguish deep, they start to sail.

The road from grief is steep and long,
Yet every step reveals their song.
In echoes soft, they find their grace,
With memories sweet, they embrace their place.

Healing blooms in tender light,
Transforming pain into sheer delight.
In every shadow, beauty grows,
From grief to grace, their spirit flows.

In the dance of time, they learn to stand,
With gentle strength, a fragile hand.
From every loss, a gift they trace,
In resilience found, from grief to grace.

Between the Cracks, I Grow

In silence I find my way,
Through shadows that softly sway.
Each crack a whisper, a gentle guide,
In solitude's arms, I learn to hide.

Roots stretch deep, unseen yet strong,
In barren soil, I still belong.
The world may judge, but I will rise,
From humble ground, I claim my prize.

With every struggle, I embrace the light,
In broken places, my soul takes flight.
There's beauty found in the strife,
Between the cracks, I nurture life.

Bridge of the Battle-Scarred

We stand on bridges, weathered and worn,
Each scar a story, a memory born.
Together we tread on this fragile span,
Bound by battles, united we stand.

The winds may howl, the storms may rage,
Yet still we walk, step by step, page by page.
Hand in hand, our spirits entwined,
On this bridge of scars, our strength defined.

Through fire and pain, we've come so far,
With every wound, we've raised a scar.
Resilience blooms where hope dared to tread,
On this bridge of battle, our dreams are fed.

Lessons from the Chasm

Deep in the chasm where shadows dance,
I gleaned the wisdom of my circumstance.
In darkness I pondered the depths of fear,
Each echo a lesson, each whisper clear.

The void teaches patience, a softer touch,
In emptiness found, I learn so much.
What's lost can lead to a brighter dawn,
From chasms emerged, a heart reborn.

As I navigate the vast unknown,
I carry the lessons the chasm has shown.
Courage grows where despair once took root,
From the depths of darkness, I now bear fruit.

Dawn's Promise after Darkness

When shadows retreat and night departs,
Dawn's gentle whispers heal our hearts.
The first light breaks, a promise anew,
With each golden ray, hope blossoms through.

In the quiet morn, we rise from the fall,
Embracing the light that beckons us all.
With every sunrise, our spirits align,
The darkness fades, and the stars resign.

A tapestry woven with hues of gold,
Stories of courage and love unfold.
As night surrenders to the warmth of day,
Dawn's promise shines, guiding our way.

Embers in the Ashes

In the quiet, whispers rise,
Softly glowing, hidden sighs.
Flickers dance through the night,
Memories burn, holding tight.

From the past, a glimmer sparks,
Lost loves echo, like small larks.
Hope reignites in darkest hours,
From desolation, springs forth flowers.

Amidst ruins, life finds way,
Even in shadows, hearts will sway.
Energies, entwined and free,
A dance of souls through mystery.

Ashes cradle the warmth inside,
We carry forth, we do not hide.
With each ember, we are reborn,
In every end, new life is sworn.

Through the embers, we reclaim,
A tapestry of love aflame.
In the night, we stand as one,
The journey starts, a new begun.

Shadows that Speak

In corners dim, the shadows sigh,
Echoes linger, as time slips by.
Stories told in whispered tones,
Breathe life into the forgotten bones.

Underneath the silver moon,
They dance softly, to a tune.
Secrets hidden, truths concealed,
In this darkness, hearts are healed.

Figures shift, then come alive,
Whispers stir, as ancients strive.
Every flicker, every shroud,
Makes the silence feel so loud.

Listen closely, they implore,
Each shadow bears a tale of yore.
Through the dusk, their voices roam,
In the night, they find a home.

Unseen bonds in twilight's grace,
In every shadow, find a place.
Through the darkness, light will seep,
For in shadows, secrets keep.

Symphony of the Broken

A fractured tune begins to play,
Melodies lost along the way.
Through the cracks, a rhythm flows,
Unraveled dreams, the heart still knows.

Each note aches, a tender sound,
In chaos, beauty can be found.
Harmony blooms from pain's embrace,
A symphony, laid bare with grace.

In the shadows, musicians weep,
Notes like raindrops, promises keep.
With every tear, the music swells,
A story woven with silent spells.

Deep within the soulful strain,
Resilience blooms from endless pain.
The world may fracture, yet we sing,
In our hearts, the hope we bring.

Among the broken, we unite,
Creating beauty in the night.
From every shard, a song will rise,
A symphony that never dies.

From Grief to Grace

In sorrow's clutch, we learn to grow,
Navigating waves, we ebb and flow.
Each tear releases what we keep,
In the silence, our hearts leap.

From the ashes of what we lose,
New beginnings bear healing hues.
Tender whispers lead the way,
Turning night into bright day.

Through the pain, we find our ground,
In darkened spaces, love is found.
Grief transforms, like morning light,
Guiding us through endless night.

With every heartbeat, hope takes flight,
From shadows deep, we seek the light.
Each step forward, a dance of grace,
Life's reflection in every face.

Holding close the joy and ache,
In the journey, hearts awake.
From grief's embers, love will blaze,
Through the struggle, find our grace.

Resurgence of the Spirit

In shadows deep, the heart will rise,
A whisper soft, beneath the skies.
Hope blooms bright, a guiding light,
Resilience wrapped in every fight.

Through trials faced, the spirit grows,
In silent strength, the courage flows.
With every tear, a seed is sown,
From ashes dark, new dreams are grown.

Yet deep within, the fire gleams,
A spark ignites forgotten dreams.
Through waves of doubt, we break the chain,
In joy's embrace, we rise again.

The path may twist, the road may bend,
But at each turn, we find a friend.
In unity, we conquer fear,
For every heart holds purpose dear.

Together we'll reclaim our grace,
In every smile, we find our place.
For in the storm, we learn to sing,
The resurgence of our spirit's spring.

Altering the Landscape of Pain

Amidst the scars, a lesson learned,
From broken paths, the heart has turned.
In shadows cast by former strife,
We carve a new way, breathe in life.

With every step, the earth reshapes,
The weight we carry, the hope escapes.
Transform the wounds to fertile ground,
In time we'll see, our strength profound.

Through every heartache, blooms the art,
Of crafting light from deep, dark parts.
We shift the view, adjust the lens,
In pain's embrace, the healing begins.

The whispers of the past, we hear,
But in their echoes, we find no fear.
For every loss, a lesson gained,
In altering pathways, we are stained.

Together we'll walk this twisted road,
In unity, we share the load.
For in the landscape drawn by grief,
We find the roots of our belief.

Building Castles from Craters

From craters deep, new visions rise,
In darkness found, a world defies.
Each jagged edge, a story tells,
Of how we thrive where sorrow dwells.

With every stone, a dream we lay,
Constructing hope, come what may.
In architect of joy and pain,
We find a way to dance in rain.

Each castle built from shattered dreams,
A fortress strong, where laughter beams.
With walls that stand against the night,
In every crack, we find our light.

Forged in the fires of our fight,
We build anew, from dark to bright.
From craters vast, our spirits soar,
In every heart, a castle's door.

So let us rise from earthen graves,
For in our strength, the future saves.
Together we create anew,
Building castles, strong and true.

Weaving Strength from Fragility

In threads of gold and silver spun,
We weave our stories, one by one.
With every strand, a gentle touch,
In fragility, we find so much.

From whispering winds, the fibers blend,
Creating strength where hearts can mend.
In quiet moments, we embrace,
The beauty found in each small space.

For every tear that stains the cloth,
A patch of light, a life enough.
In woven tales of sorrow's flight,
Emerges hope, a guiding light.

Together now, we shape the loom,
Transforming fears, dispelling gloom.
With every knot, our spirits soar,
Weave strength anew, forever more.

In unity, our fabric grows,
Through fragile threads, a truth bestows.
For in the heart of every seam,
We weave the strength of every dream.

Phoenix in the Night

From ashes cold, it starts to rise,
A flame reborn beneath the skies.
In midnight's cloak, it finds its flight,
A fierce resolve to claim the night.

With wings of fire that grace the air,
It dances high, no trace of care.
Each spark a story, old yet true,
A legacy of vibrant hue.

The shadows fade as feathers glow,
In radiance, its spirit flows.
For every end, a brand new start,
The phoenix lives within the heart.

Through trials faced and battles fought,
It teaches us what can't be taught.
Embrace the fire, let it soar,
In darkest times, it screams for more.

So fear not night, for light shall come,
The phoenix sings, a vibrant hum.
With every challenge, rise and shine,
For in the dark, your flame will line.

Radiance after the Rain

The clouds disperse, the sun breaks through,
A gentle warmth, a golden hue.
Each droplet sparkles, fresh and bright,
A world reborn, pure and light.

With every petal kissed by dew,
The earth awakens, fresh and new.
The colors dance, a vibrant chorus,
In nature's arms, we find our solace.

A rainbow arcs across the sky,
Whispering dreams that soar and fly.
The air is sweet, the heart feels free,
In beauty's grace, we yearn to be.

So let the storm wash doubts away,
Embrace the light, come what may.
With every struggle, strength unfolds,
In radiance, our story holds.

After the rain, hope's bloom ignites,
A testament to endless sights.
Together we'll chase every beam,
In unity, we'll live the dream.

Grit Beneath the Surface

Beneath the waves, the currents churn,
Deep in the ground, the embers burn.
In silent strength, the roots entwine,
A testament to grit divine.

Underneath, a world awaits,
With stories locked behind the gates.
The stones may seem so rough and cold,
Yet, in their heart, a truth unfolds.

Against the odds, they stand and fight,
Unyielding spirit, pure and bright.
For in the dark, resilience grows,
A strength that only nature knows.

From dirt and stone, the flowers bloom,
Transforming life in every room.
In struggle's arms, we learn to thrive,
For in our grit, we come alive.

So treasure hardship, let it teach,
For through the struggle, we shall reach.
With every step, we find our way,
The grit we hold will guide each day.

Chasing the Light Within

In quiet corners, whispers sing,
Awakening truths like early spring.
Each heartbeat echoes with a call,
To find the light that lives in all.

Through shadows deep, we search and strive,
For hidden sparks that make us thrive.
In every dream, a glimmer lies,
A beacon bright beneath the skies.

With courage bold, we break the chains,
Unraveling joy, despite the pains.
For hope is found in tender ways,
That guide us through the darkest days.

So trust the voice that stirs your soul,
For in its warmth, we become whole.
With every step, the light draws near,
In chasing dreams, we conquer fear.

Embrace the journey, seek the spark,
In every shadow, find the mark.
For when we chase what lies within,
We light the world, let love begin.

Mending the Frayed Edges

In twilight's gentle embrace,
Threads of hope begin to intertwine.
Stitching hearts with silent grace,
Lost dreams rise, and stars align.

Whispers of the past still echo,
Each tear a tale, each scar a song.
Through the cracks, new light shall flow,
Binding wounds, where we belong.

With every knot, our spirits bloom,
In the fabric of the night,
Together we weave away the gloom,
In unity, we claim our light.

Hands that tremble, souls that mend,
In the tapestry of time, we stand.
Each moment shared is a gift we send,
Stitched with love, forever planned.

So let us gather, stitch by stitch,
In every fiber, we find our way.
Mending edges, quiet but rich,
In the warmth of hope, we'll stay.

Beyond the Tempest

Beneath the stormy skies we tread,
Winds of chaos lash and roar.
Yet through the fear, our hearts are led,
To seek the calm on a distant shore.

Waves may crash, but spirits rise,
In every trial, we find our strength.
Through the darkness, hope defies,
And guides us forward, mile by length.

After the storm, a vibrant hue,
The sun breaks forth, the clouds depart.
With every dawn, the world feels new,
Echoes of courage fill our heart.

In the aftermath, we gather stones,
Each a lesson, each a prayer.
Building bridges from our bones,
Finding peace beyond despair.

So sail we must, on waters wide,
With sails of dreams, we'll dare to roam.
For after the tempest, love will guide,
To shores where weary souls call home.

An Odyssey of Renewal

In the quiet dawn we start to rise,
With dreams as bright as morning dew.
For every journey holds a prize,
As we embrace the old and new.

With every step, we shed the past,
Breaking chains that held us tight.
In the rush of waves, we're cast,
Finding our way towards the light.

The road is long, but hearts are brave,
Each moment rich with promise sweet.
Through every storm, we learn to save
The fragments of our bittersweet.

With voices joined, we sing our song,
In harmony, we find our way.
Together, where we all belong,
Through shadows thick, we greet the day.

So let us wander, souls reborn,
Embracing life, both wild and free.
With every dawn, new visions torn,
An odyssey of renewal, we decree.

Transcending the Tides

Upon the shore, where waters meet,
The ebb and flow of time holds true.
Each wave a whisper, soft and sweet,
Carrying dreams, both old and new.

Beneath the moon's gentle embrace,
We dance with shadows, light, and spray.
In every ripple, we find our place,
In the ocean's heart, we long to stay.

Time may shift on currents wide,
Yet souls entwined shall stand the test.
In tides of change, we find our guide,
Rising up, we are truly blessed.

Through storms we brave, with hearts like fire,
We forge our path against the tide.
With every surge, we seek desire,
In the sea's depths, our truths abide.

So let us sail on waters deep,
Transcending fears, with courage bold.
In unity, our promises we keep,
Embracing all that life has told.

Beauty Born of Despair

In shadows deep where silence grows,
A fragile light begins to glow.
From tears that fall like heavy rain,
A heart can rise from weary pain.

Through broken dreams and silent nights,
We weave the darkness into sights.
From every hurt, a story told,
In wounds, we find the strength of gold.

With every scar, a tale we bear,
In sorrow's arms, we learn to care.
The beauty found in every tear,
Transforms the pain, makes love sincere.

So let the shadows gently caress,
For in their depths, we find our best.
A symphony of hope and dread,
In every note, new life is bred.

From ashes rise the blooms of grace,
In every struggle, we find our place.
What seems like loss can help us grow,
In every crack, the light can flow.

The Fire that Forged Us

In flames that dance, our spirits soar,
Each trial fierce, a raging war.
Through searing heat, we learn to bend,
A stronger bond, a journey's end.

The embers glow of cherished dreams,
In unity, our courage beams.
With hearts ablaze, we face the night,
Together bold, we ignite the light.

Through tempests wild, we find our ground,
In every roar, a voice profound.
The furnace tests, but makes us whole,
In every scar, we find our soul.

For every spark that lights the way,
Reminds us of our fierce display.
In shadows cast by flames so bright,
We forged a path, we wrote our fight.

The trials faced, the fears embraced,
In fire's forge, our lives are laced.
Emerging strong, we stand as one,
In unity, our battles won.

Transcending the Tempest

In raging storms where hope seems lost,
We sail the waves at any cost.
With winds that howl and skies of gray,
We find our way, come what may.

The thunder roars, a fearsome sound,
Yet in the chaos, strength is found.
Through torrents fierce, we learn to glide,
With every rise, we swallow pride.

As lightning strikes and shadows loom,
We gather light to chase the gloom.
With hearts entwined, we dance the rain,
In every drop, we break the chain.

Above the storm, a sun will break,
A promise whispered in our wake.
Transcending trials, we learn to fly,
With wings of hope, we touch the sky.

In tempests wild, we find our voice,
In every struggle, we rejoice.
Together strong, we face the rush,
Transforming pain into the hush.

Cracked but Not Broken

In every crack, the light shines through,
A testament to what we knew.
For every flaw, a grace embraced,
In every mark, our lives interlaced.

The moments spent in shadows cast,
Remind us that no storm can last.
Through fractured paths, we learn to stand,
With open hearts and steady hands.

Though battered souls and weary eyes,
In brokenness, our strength can rise.
We weave our tales, both harsh and sweet,
In every loss, a chance to meet.

With jagged edges, we create,
A mosaic rich, we celebrate.
Embracing scars, we find our worth,
In every bruise, a chance for mirth.

So let the world see all we are,
In every crack, a guiding star.
For we are strong, though life may shake,
In every piece, we're not forsake.

Reclaiming the Lost Dreams

In the depths of the night sky,
Flickers of hopes long gone by.
Whispers of wishes softly call,
To revive the spirits of all.

Dusty pathways we once roamed,
Searching for the seeds we've sown.
Awakening visions, bright and clear,
Resurge the dreams we hold dear.

The silence sings a soothing tune,
As shadows dance beneath the moon.
Each heartbeat echoes with intent,
For dreams once lost, now heaven-sent.

Behind the clouds, a light appears,
Washing away forgotten fears.
With faith as our guiding light,
We reclaim our dreams, take flight.

In unity, we strive and rise,
As ambition fills the skies.
Together we chase the unseen beams,
Reclaiming our lost, cherished dreams.

Awakening from Ashes

From the embers, a flicker glows,
A promise of life beneath the woes.
Silent shadows, hear our plea,
Awakening strength to set us free.

The weight of silence, heavy still,
But within us stirs an iron will.
Resilience wrapped in tender grace,
A spirit reborn, a vibrant place.

What once was lost now finds its way,
In the dawn of a brand new day.
With every breath, we ignite the spark,
Emerging bold from the dark.

Across the ruins of yesterday's fight,
A vision born from black to light.
Through trials endured, we emerge pure,
Awakening hearts that love endures.

From ashes rise, the phoenix sings,
Carrying hope on radiant wings.
In the cycle of life, we find our glow,
Awakening the power we sow.

The Strength of Shadows

In twilight's embrace, shadows sway,
Guardians of dreams that drift away.
Whispered secrets of the night,
Hold the wisdom, fierce and bright.

With every dusk, they weave a tale,
In the silence, their voices prevail.
Strength lies buried, hidden, deep,
In the shadows, their promises keep.

Cloaked in the whispers of despair,
A resilient spirit lingers there.
For even darkness holds a spark,
Creating light when we embark.

Through haunting echoes, we find our way,
Learning from shadows, come what may.
In their depths, we gather strength,
Embracing life in all its lengths.

So dance with shadows, embrace their grace,
In darkness, we find our rightful place.
For every fear we learn to face,
The strength of shadows, our sacred space.

Soaring from Sorrow

In the valley where shadows meet,
Sorrow whispers in refrain so sweet.
Yet within the heart, a flickering flame,
Ignites the spirit, calls my name.

A heavy cloud can veil the sun,
But still we rise when day is done.
With every tear that blends with rain,
We find the strength to break the chain.

In the echoes of pain, a lesson blooms,
Turning sorrow into vibrant tunes.
With every struggle, a chance to mend,
Soaring high as the heart can bend.

Lifted by wings of hope and light,
We transcend the darkness, enter night.
Through the storms, we embrace the flight,
Soaring from sorrow, embracing the height.

With every dawn, we understand,
That from despair, we're never banned.
For in our hearts, the truth will sing,
Soaring above, on freedom's wing.

Rebirth in the Ruins

Among the ashes, life finds a way,
Roots creep forth, in the light of day.
A tender shoot breaks barren ground,
Hope in silence, where lost is found.

Whispers of change in the gentle breeze,
Nature's balm heals, brings heart to ease.
Crumbled walls, yet beauty blooms,
In every shadow, a future looms.

Fallen stones weave tales of old,
In the quiet, stories unfold.
A vibrant heart beats through the pain,
From brokenness, growth shall reign.

The past remains, a distant ghost,
Yet from the ruins, we can boast.
Of life renewed in every crevice,
A testament to our own tenacity.

So let us rise, like the phoenix strong,
In the whispers of night, we belong.
Fear fades away as dawn draws near,
In the ruins, hope is crystal clear.

Embracing the Thunder

When clouds gather and shadows play,
Lightning dances, wild and gray.
Embrace the storm, let it roar,
In chaos, find what you adore.

The sky rumbles, a curious sound,
In the tempest tall, strength is found.
With every strike, fear takes flight,
A symphony born from the night.

Through pouring rain and fierce delight,
The heart opens to the fright.
Awakening dreams that once lay still,
In the storm's embrace, all is thrill.

Hands reach high to catch the flare,
A dance of courage, raw and rare.
Together we rise, hearts aligned,
In thunder's grip, we are defined.

So when the skies begin to shout,
Stand tall, release all doubt.
Embrace the thunder, let it sing,
For in its arms, we find our wing.

Shattered, Yet Whole

Fragments linger in the light,
Scattered pieces, a daunting sight.
Yet within chaos, beauty stays,
Each shard reflects our myriad ways.

Pain carves lines, like scars on skin,
Stories written, where we've been.
A mosaic crafted from our strife,
Each break a chapter of our life.

The heart can crack but not be lost,
In vulnerability, we pay the cost.
Edges rough yet soft within,
From shattered past, our souls begin.

Embracing flaws, letting go,
In every fissure, beauty flows.
Together we stand, imperfectly bold,
In the tapestry of life, we unfold.

So gather the pieces, don't be afraid,
In unity woven, we are remade.
Shattered, yet whole, we rise anew,
In all of our flaws, we find what's true.

The Alchemy of Hurt

From bitter roots, sweet flowers bloom,
In the depths of pain, we find our room.
With every tear, a lesson learned,
In scars of time, strength is earned.

Gold is forged in the fire's dance,
Through trials endured, we take a chance.
Transmute the hurt, let it refine,
In shadows, our spirits align.

As darkness whispers, listen close,
For from our fears, we find the most.
Alchemy turns our wounds to gold,
In the heart's furnace, courage bold.

We rise like phoenix from the ash,
Transforming sorrow into a splash.
A canvas painted by each scar,
In the silence, we become our star.

So cherish the pain, let it teach,
In every bruise, wisdom's reach.
The alchemy of hurt is real and true,
In every heartbreak, we are renewed.

From Fracture to Flight

In shadows deep, the heart lies still,
Cracks embrace, the void to fill.
Yet in the dark, a spark ignites,
From fractured ground, the spirit fights.

Wings unfold from pain's tight grasp,
Transcending limits, fate's warm clasp.
With every tear, the soul takes flight,
Emerging bold, into the light.

A journey wrought from broken dreams,
Each scar a tale, or so it seems.
To rise anew, the past we greet,
With strength restored, we find our feet.

Embrace the hurt, let echoes fade,
In every fall, a chance is made.
The sky invites, the heart shall soar,
From fracture deep, we learn to roar.

With hope aglow, the path now clear,
From heavy chains, we shed the fear.
For through the storm we find our way,
From fracture's grasp, we greet the day.

Blossoms in the Bruise

Beneath the weight of silent cries,
Life finds a way beneath the skies.
In every bruise, a tale unfolds,
Of strength and beauty, fierce and bold.

Petals push through the cracked hard ground,
In darkest nights, sweet hope is found.
For every wound that life can bring,
Unfurling joy, the heart will sing.

The garden blooms from bitter strife,
Resilience shines, a dance of life.
With every crack, the colors burst,
In bruises deep, the blossoms thirst.

Each thorn that pricks, each sorrow's mark,
Breeds flowers bright, igniting spark.
The art of growth from pain so rife,
In shadows deep, we find the life.

So cherish scars, they shape the whole,
In every bruise, the strength of soul.
For from the hurt, the flowers rise,
In nature's dance, the spirit flies.

Echoes of Resilience

In quiet whispers, strength resounds,
Through trials faced, the heart rebounds.
With every echo, stories share,
Of storms endured and love laid bare.

In shadows' hold, the spirit grows,
Amidst the strife, a bloom bestows.
With courage sewn in every seam,
We weave our hopes into a dream.

Resilience sings in every thread,
A tapestry from tears we shed.
The past, though heavy, does not bind,
For freedom lives within the mind.

Through tempests fierce, we learn to dance,
In every stumble, find our chance.
With echoes ringing, hearts unite,
We rise again, reclaim our light.

So let the echoes guide the way,
Through darkest nights and brightest day.
In unity, we stand, we thrive,
With echoes proud, we come alive.

The Art of Unbreaking

In every fracture, art is found,
Life's masterpiece on broken ground.
With colors wild, we paint the pain,
Transforming loss with every gain.

Through shattered glass, the light will shine,
Creating beauty, bold design.
For in the cracks, we find a voice,
In every wound, a wiser choice.

To mend the heart, to shape anew,
The art of love in all we do.
Each piece a story, woven tight,
In hands of grace, we find the might.

With every stitch, the fabric grows,
A quilt of dreams, in warmth bestows.
From brokenness, a stronger self,
A living art, beyond the shelf.

So let us turn our scars to art,
In every ending, a brand new start.
For in unbreaking, life takes flight,
A canvas bright, adorned with light.

Fragments of Hope

In shadows dark, a flicker glows,
A gentle breeze, where courage flows.
Each step we take, the path unfolds,
In whispered dreams, our heart beholds.

Through tangled fears, we seek the light,
In broken dreams, the stars burn bright.
With every tear, a story we weave,
In the silence, we shall believe.

The distant echo of a hopeful song,
Reminds us here, we still belong.
From ashes rise, our spirits soar,
In unity, we are never poor.

The trembling hands find strength within,
A tapestry of hope begins.
With love as thread, we sew our fate,
In fragments, still, we celebrate.

Together we dance, we laugh, we cry,
In every loss, a reason why.
For in the shards, the future gleams,
In fragments, still, we find our dreams.

A Journey from Darkness

Once lost in shadows, I wandered deep,
Through valleys low, where silence keeps.
With heavy heart, I faced the night,
Yet felt within, a spark of light.

With every step, the darkness waned,
In broken paths, my soul was trained.
A guiding star, though faint and far,
Illuminated who we are.

Through tangled woods, I found my voice,
In whispers soft, I made my choice.
To rise beyond the chains that bind,
To leave the past, the fear behind.

With open heart, I met the dawn,
In every breath, a strength reborn.
Through trials worn, my spirit soared,
For in the light, I am restored.

The road ahead, with stones and fears,
With time I'll mend these broken years.
And in the journey, I shall find,
A future bright, a heart aligned.

The Art of Healing

In tender hands, we learn to mend,
A gentle touch, a faithful friend.
With every breath, a chance to grow,
In patience found, the love will flow.

From ashes stirred, we craft a dream,
In shattered pieces, we build a theme.
With colors bright, we paint the scars,
In whispered hopes, we reach for stars.

In silence deep, the heart can speak,
In listening ears, we find the weak.
Each story told, a bridge we make,
In shared lives lived, our hearts awake.

With open arms, we bear the weight,
Transforming pain into something great.
Through every tear, a lesson learned,
In healing's art, our spirits turned.

Together we heal, no heart alone,
In the dance of life, love is our tone.
And through the storms, we hold on tight,
In the art of healing, we find the light.

When Thunder Becomes Light

In stormy skies, the thunder rolls,
A symphony of troubled souls.
Yet in the clash, we find our fire,
A dance of hope, a fierce desire.

The rain may fall, the winds may howl,
But in the chaos, we will prowl.
For every flash, a truth revealed,
In darkness faced, our hearts are healed.

When shadows creep, and fear takes flight,
Through lightning strikes, we chase the night.
With every roar, the soul ignites,
In tempest's grip, we claim our rights.

Through whispered winds, a promise made,
That after darkness, light won't fade.
In every storm, a chance to rise,
When thunder roars, we'll reach the skies.

So let the storms come, let them rage,
For in the clash, we turn the page.
When thunder fades, we'll stand apart,
As light emerges, bold and smart.

Through Shadows into Light

In the depths where fears reside,
Dreamers whisper, hearts collide.
Hope ignites a fragile flame,
Leading souls beyond the same.

Rays of dawn break through the gray,
Chasing all our doubts away.
Every step, a brightening sight,
Through the shadows into light.

Voices rise, a hopeful song,
Together we are brave and strong.
Facing trials, we unite,
Through the shadows into light.

Broken chains and lifted heads,
From the ashes, purpose spreads.
With each battle, fear takes flight,
Through the shadows into light.

Let us dance, and let us sing,
For tomorrow's endless spring.
Hand in hand, our spirits bright,
Through the shadows into light.

The Colors of Survival

In every heartbeat, shades of pain,
The vibrant hues of love remain.
Every struggle, every fight,
Paints a canvas bold and bright.

Through the storms, where hope feels thin,
We find the strength that lives within.
Each brushstroke writes a story true,
The colors of survival view.

Blues of sorrow, reds of fire,
Greens of growth, we transpire.
In every tear, in every cheer,
The colors of survival clear.

With every wound and every scar,
We find our way, we reach the star.
Together in this vibrant hue,
The colors of survival, we pursue.

Let passion guide us through the night,
With every color, find our light.
In every heart, a piece anew,
The colors of survival, true.

Hearts in the Storm

Beneath the clouds, our spirits rise,
With thunder's roar and whispered sighs.
Together we stand, hand in hand,
Hearts in the storm, we take a stand.

Raindrops fall like dreams once lost,
But we embrace the pain, the cost.
In tempests fierce, we find our way,
Hearts in the storm, come what may.

Lightning strikes, our fears ignite,
Yet still we seek the silver light.
Together we face the raging night,
Hearts in the storm, ready to fight.

Through the chaos, our voices blend,
In the wild, our hearts transcend.
Every crack, a chance to sway,
Hearts in the storm, come what may.

When calm returns, we've forged a bond,
In every tempest, we respond.
Stronger now, we'll find our way,
Hearts in the storm, here to stay.

Songs of Unyielding Souls

In the quiet, a gentle tune,
Voices rise like flowers bloom.
From the depths, our spirits sing,
Songs of unyielding souls take wing.

With every note, a tale unfolds,
Of battles fought, of dreams retold.
Together we share the melody,
Songs of unyielding souls, so free.

Through the valleys, our voices soar,
Echoes of hope forevermore.
With each harmony, we shall grow,
Songs of unyielding souls, aglow.

In the darkness, the light remains,
Music heals our deepest pains.
Joining hearts, we write our scroll,
Songs of unyielding souls, our goal.

Set to rhythms, we will rise,
Painting dreams across the skies.
With every heartbeat, once more,
Songs of unyielding souls restore.

Metamorphosis of the Soul

In shadows deep, the spirit stirs,
Awakening truths, it softly purrs.
From ashes rise, a golden hue,
Rebirth unfolds, each day anew.

Through trials faced, the soul takes flight,
In search of wisdom, draped in light.
The chrysalis breaks, revealing grace,
Transcending time, a sacred space.

Each heartbeat sings, a song of change,
Embracing all, though feelings strange.
In every tear, a lesson learned,
The fires burn, yet hope is turned.

With open arms, the journey calls,
In knowing love, the spirit falls.
Emerging strong, from fears released,
The metamorphosis, a heart unleashed.

Floating dreams on wings so bright,
Eclipsing dark to bring forth light.
The soul will dance, with sheer delight,
In wonder's grace, we take to flight.

The Well of Sleep-worn Dreams

In whispers soft, the night unfolds,
Where sleep-worn dreams, their tales retold.
The stars align, in velvet skies,
A well of thoughts, beneath resides.

Each droplet shines, a wish awaits,
A journey bold, through hidden gates.
In shadows spun, our visions clear,
The echoes of the heart draw near.

To wander lost, through realms unseen,
With every breath, we drift between.
A tapestry of hopes and fears,
Woven tight through all our years.

In silence holds, the dreams unique,
A whispered prayer that none can speak.
To taste the light, that flickers still,
A well of love, a gentle thrill.

As dawn breaks through, the visions fade,
But in our hearts, they're softly laid.
The well remains, a sacred place,
Where dreams abide in soft embrace.

Kintsugi of the Heart

In cracks and seams, the beauty lies,
A broken past, where hope complies.
With golden threads, we mend the scars,
In every fault, a glimpse of stars.

The heart once shattered, now a blend,
Of joy and pain, a gentle mend.
In every flaw, a story told,
In fragile hands, the warmth of gold.

Through storms we face, we learn to grow,
In every crack, the light will show.
The art of love, with tender grace,
A journey shared, our sacred space.

With open wounds, we rise anew,
In every piece, a stronger view.
The heart transformed, its spirit bold,
In Kintsugi's hands, our truths unfold.

Embrace the scars, for they will sing,
Of all the love that life can bring.
In golden seams, our hearts collide,
In this sweet dance, we will abide.

Stories Woven in Wounds

In every scar, a tale is spun,
Of battles fought, a race we've run.
The fabric frayed, yet threads still gleam,
In wounded hearts, we find our dream.

Through darkest nights, we weave the light,
With every tear, new hope ignites.
The stories told, in whispered sighs,
Of love and loss, where courage lies.

The wounds remind us of our strength,
As we embrace the road's great length.
Each mark upon our skin will show,
The stories shared, that help us grow.

In healing hands, we start anew,
With every thread, a hue so true.
Through pain expressed, the heart will mend,
In weaving tales, we learn to bend.

For wounds may fade, yet stories flow,
In every heart, a river's glow.
The fabric of our lives entwined,
In wounds we find the ties that bind.

Scars as Stories

Each scar a tale, a whispered fight,
Time's gentle brush, both dark and light.
Stories etched upon my skin,
A legacy forged through loss and win.

Every mark, a lesson learned,
With every tear, my spirit burned.
A canvas of battles, a silent cry,
In every scar, a piece of why.

Memories linger, shadows dance,
In pain, I found a second chance.
With grace I wear each line, each trace,
A testament of strength and grace.

I stand adorned in history's art,
Every wound has played its part.
Embracing stories, old yet new,
Each scar a marker of what's true.

Through storms I've wandered, unafraid,
In shadows deep, my spirit swayed.
A tapestry woven, brave and bold,
In every scar, a story told.

Blossoms in the Ruins

In crumbled stones, new life breaks free,
Amidst the dust, nature's decree.
Petals soft against the stone,
Resilience blooms in places alone.

With every crack, the sun's embrace,
Hope finds a path, a sacred space.
Through shattered dreams, a fragrance spreads,
A testament to what still bled.

Among the ruins, colors ignite,
Beauty bursts forth, a stunning sight.
Life persists where pain once dwelt,
In the silence, strength is felt.

Sheltered whispers in gentle winds,
The past has shaped, but not rescinds.
From ashes rise the boldest hues,
In fractured soil, the world renews.

Blossoms sway in tender grace,
Holding onto their rightful place.
In every tear, a seed was sown,
A reminder that we're never alone.

The Unseen Climb

In shadows deep, the journey starts,
One step forward, heavy hearts.
Mountains loom, yet hope's a spark,
Guiding souls through paths so dark.

With every stumble, strength ignites,
Under stars, we chase the lights.
Each breath a promise, slow but sure,
In the unseen, we will endure.

Fingers grasp at dreams so high,
The summit whispers, never shy.
Through aching limbs and weary minds,
Clarity waits, true peace unwinds.

Courage swells as fears release,
With every hardship comes sweet peace.
A mountain forged by grit and will,
Ascending paths, embrace the thrill.

The climb may hide, yet we will find,
In every shadow, love is kind.
Step by step, our spirits soar,
Through unseen heights, we seek for more.

Resilient Heartbeats

In the quiet, hear the drum,
A heartbeat's echo, steady, numb.
Through trials faced, the rhythm grows,
In every struggle, resilience flows.

Pulses strong amid the strife,
Echoing the strength of life.
With every beat, tales unfold,
A story woven, brave and bold.

In moments faint, a spark ignites,
Guiding through the darkest nights.
When hope feels lost, just breathe in deep,
In every heartbeat, dreams still leap.

Together we rise, hand in hand,
A symphony of hearts, we stand.
With every pulse, new dreams ignite,
Resilient spirits take to flight.

In every challenge, we unite,
A dance of souls, an endless flight.
Through ups and downs, we claim the day,
In resilient heartbeats, we find our way.

Embracing the Unknown

In shadows deep where secrets lie,
We wander forth, with hearts held high.
The path unknown, it calls our name,
In leaps of faith, we stake our claim.

With every step, we shed the doubt,
A world unseen, we're drawn about.
The winding road, it twists and turns,
In every challenge, a lesson learns.

Though fear may loom, we stand as one,
Together strong, we'll face the sun.
For in the dark, a spark will glow,
Embracing all that we don't know.

Threads of Tenacity

In tapestry of dreams we weave,
With threads of hope, we will believe.
Each knot a story, twisted tight,
Together we'll shine, a guiding light.

Through storms we'll sail, the winds will howl,
But in our hearts, we wear the crown.
Resilience strong, like steel it bends,
In every struggle, a strength ascends.

With every tear, a thread will glow,
In woven patterns, our spirits grow.
For every trial, we stand our ground,
In unity, our voices sound.

The Dance of the Undaunted

We rise with grace, on trembling ground,
In every step, our fears are drowned.
With fierce resolve, we take our stance,
In rhythms bold, we find our dance.

The night may fall, the shadows creep,
But in our hearts, a fire we keep.
Through trials faced, we'll find our way,
In every heartbeat, hope will stay.

With daring flames, we spark the night,
In every twirl, we chase the light.
For undaunted souls, the music plays,
In every moment, courage sways.

Embracing the Fire Within

A flicker starts, a blaze will rise,
In depths of heart, our passion lies.
With every spark, we light the sky,
Embracing fire, we soar so high.

Through trials faced, we stoke the flame,
In warmth of spirit, we claim our name.
With open hearts, we face the storm,
In blazing truth, our souls transform.

For in the heat, our strength ignites,
We burn so bright, through darkest nights.
Embracing all that we have sought,
With fire within, our battles fought.

From Silence into Sound

Whispers of night fade away,
Echoes of dawn, bright and clear.
Notes dance lightly in the air,
Melodies rise, washing all fear.

Voices of hope blend and twine,
Harmonies burst, claiming their place.
Every heart joins in the song,
Creating a world filled with grace.

Gentle rains tap on the ground,
Nature's rhythm, pure and profound.
In this moment, joy is found,
From silence, a symphony bound.

Joyful laughter fills the streets,
Children play, their spirits soar.
Life's whispers turn to sweet beats,
In every heart, longing for more.

So let us sing, let voices blend,
Unite in harmony, hearts to mend.
From silence, we rise, one and all,
In the embrace of sound, we stand tall.

Celebrating the Courageous

Bold souls stride, fearless and bright,
Facing the storms with steady gaze.
Through darkest days, they bring light,
In every heart, their spirit stays.

With every challenge, they stand proud,
A tapestry of strength and grace.
From silent shadows, they emerge loud,
Defying fate, they find their place.

Resilient hearts, they rise and fight,
Turning the tide with steadfast will.
Each wound, a mark of their might,
With every step, their dreams fulfill.

In moments tough, they do not yield,
Courage blooms in fields of pain.
Through sacrifice, their fate is sealed,
A triumph born from every strain.

We gather now to raise our cheers,
To those who brave the tempest's call.
In celebration, we shed our fears,
For courage shines in one and all.

A Journey of Unfolding

Step by step, the path reveals,
Wonders waiting, softly calling.
In every stride, a story heals,
The heart awakens, freely sprawling.

With every dawn, new dreams arise,
The map of life unfolds with grace.
Through twist and turn, there's no disguise,
In journeys shared, we find our place.

Each moment lived is a treasure,
A tapestry woven with care.
In laughter, love, and all the pleasure,
Connections flourish, hearts laid bare.

Mountains high and rivers wide,
The landscape shifts, an endless song.
Through every ebb, we learn to glide,
A dance of life where all belong.

As petals bloom and seasons change,
So do we, with every breath.
In this journey, nothing is strange,
For in love, we conquer death.

The Triumph of Tenacity

In the face of trials, they rise,
With grit and grace, they press on through.
Beyond the struggle, clear blue skies,
A testament to all they do.

Each setback met with fierce resolve,
As mountains crumble, they stand tall.
In every challenge, strength evolves,
Through storms, they answer the call.

With hands held high, they lift their voices,
Bound by dreams, they journey forth.
In the dance of fate, they make choices,
Turning despair into rebirth.

Tenacity shines like the sun,
Warming hearts in winter's chill.
In every battle bravely won,
They forge ahead with steadfast will.

So let us honor their fierce fight,
A chorus rising, loud and clear.
For in their story burns a light,
The triumph of tenacity we revere.

The Echo of Every Battle

In the silence of the night,
Shadows whisper tales of fight.
Memories of courage, bold and bright,
Echoes linger, take their flight.

Each clash, a heartbeat, fierce and loud,
Voices rise above the crowd.
From ashes, rise, then stand unbowed,
These warriors wear their honor proud.

With every step upon the ground,
A legacy is tightly wound.
In each heart, a fervor found,
Resilience blooms where hope is crowned.

Though wounds may ache and time may sting,
The heart remembers everything.
Like ancient trees in whispers sing,
The echo of each battle's ring.

So stand we tall and face the dawn,
With every dusk, a new light's drawn.
For in the fight, we find our song,
In echoes of the brave, we long.

Hearts Forged in Fire

From molten streams, our spirits rise,
Forged in flames, beneath the skies.
With every trial, the heart complies,
In searing heat, our passion flies.

Anvil strong, we shape our fate,
In moments bitter, love creates.
With every clash, we elevate,
Hearts entwined, a burning state.

Together we endure the blaze,
Through swirling smoke, we spark a craze.
In darkness cloaked, still brightly gaze,
Hearts ignited in fiery haze.

With every tear, a light ignites,
In shadows deep, we find our sights.
From embers glows our shared delights,
Through trials faced, our love ignites.

So here's to hearts that stand the heat,
In life's great forge, we rise, complete.
With every challenge, never beat,
Together strong, our love's heartbeat.

Fragments Turned into Flight

Broken pieces, scattered wide,
In chaos, dreams and hopes reside.
Yet from the shards, a spark inside,
Transforms the pain, a daring ride.

With each fragment, stories weave,
Resilience found, we dare believe.
As we transform, we take our leave,
From shadows, now, we brightly cleave.

Through storms we gather strength anew,
In the winds, our spirits grew.
From ruins left, we boldly flew,
In every heart, a world in view.

Embracing light, we share our song,
From every crack, where we belong.
In unity, we rise, so strong,
Turning fragments into flight along.

So dance within the skies above,
With wings of hope, with hearts of love.
In every leap, we find and prove,
That fragments soared, the world we shove.

Unseen Wings

In twilight's hush, the whispers soar,
A gentle breeze behind the door.
With unseen wings, we start to explore,
The paths of dreams we've not dared before.

With every breath, a secret held,
In silence deep, our spirits meld.
Through shadows cast, our courage swelled,
With unseen wings, our fates expelled.

We rise above, though trials bend,
In quiet strength, our hearts ascend.
With every twist, the journey's blend,
Unseen wings, on which we depend.

They carry whispers of the night,
In hidden realms, we find our light.
Through darkest hours, they bring delight,
With unseen wings, we take our flight.

So trust the path that lies ahead,
With every step, lose fear and dread.
Unseen wings lead where we are led,
In dreams and hopes, our hearts are fed.

Milton Keynes UK
Ingram Content Group UK Ltd.
UKHW022223251124
451566UK00006B/92